A Colouring Book of Hours:

CASTLE

by the hand of
Marcia Overstrand

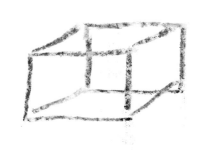

~To **Kenii**~

A Colouring Book of Hours:
CASTLE

by the hand of

Marcia Overstrand
and

Angie Sage

SEPTIMUS
PRESS
❖
the home of
good books
❖

☆ Happy colouring ! ☆

Published by Septimus Press

A Colouring Book of Hours: CASTLE
Interior art copyright © 2015 Angie Sage

First edition
1 3 5 7 9 8 6 4 2

for further information: www.septimus-press.com

Printed by The Gomer Press, Llandysul, Ceredigion, Wales
for Septimus Press Ltd.

ISBN 978-0-9934362-0-8

9 780993 436208

Vistas and Vignettes

A Colouring Book of Hours is printed on special paper that allows you to use your favourite pens, crayons or paints without the colour bleeding beyond where it is wanted, and without raising fibres from the surface. Unless you are using marker pens, it won't show through on the other side of the paper either.

If you want to be sure, the last page has a space where you can try out your pens.

You can also use watercolour paints, and some people like water colour crayons: a dab of water applied with a fine brush really makes the colours glow, and you can also blend them. Best to let the pages dry, though, before you close the book.

Welcome to the Castle

Come for a few minutes' respite, or even better spend the day here.

Rise with the lark, dip into the morning pool, wander through the labyrynth to the cloud pavilion and stroll along the lantern path.

A hidden doorway takes you to the alchemist's alcove and after a visit to the shell grotto, lunch will be set out for you.

Enjoy the river walk, discover the boathouse folly and luxuriate in the closet of silks.

It's getting late now and the evening library beckons. Watch the moon rise, then take the night stairs to the second-best bed.

And what of the best bed? You'll have to imagine that: some things Marcia doesn't tell.

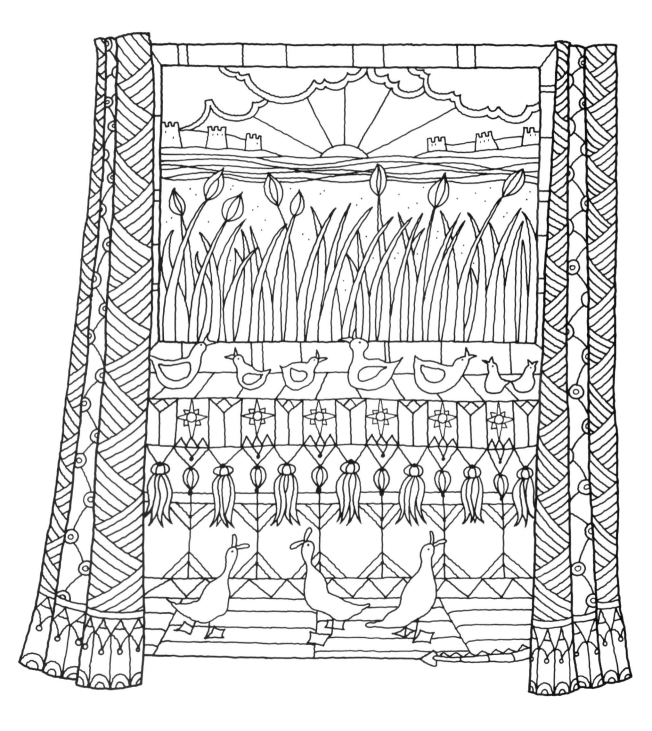

~The Dawn Singers~

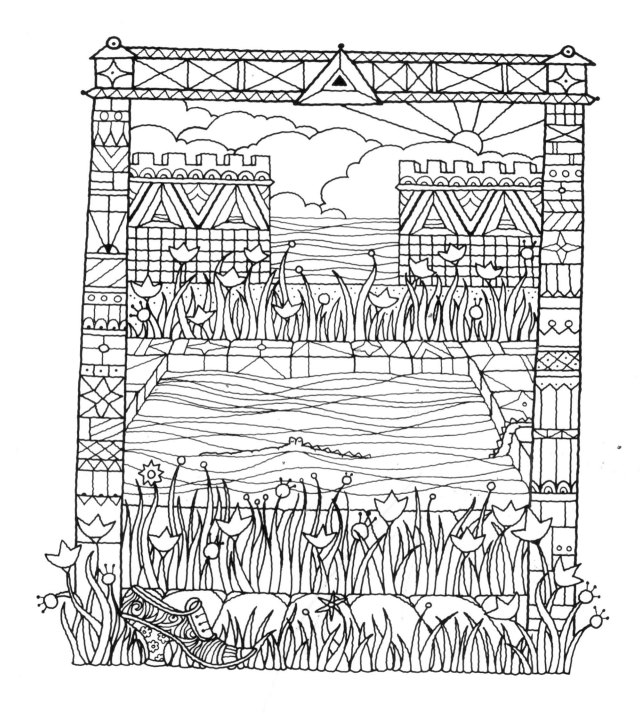

The Morning Pool

The Labyrinth Summit

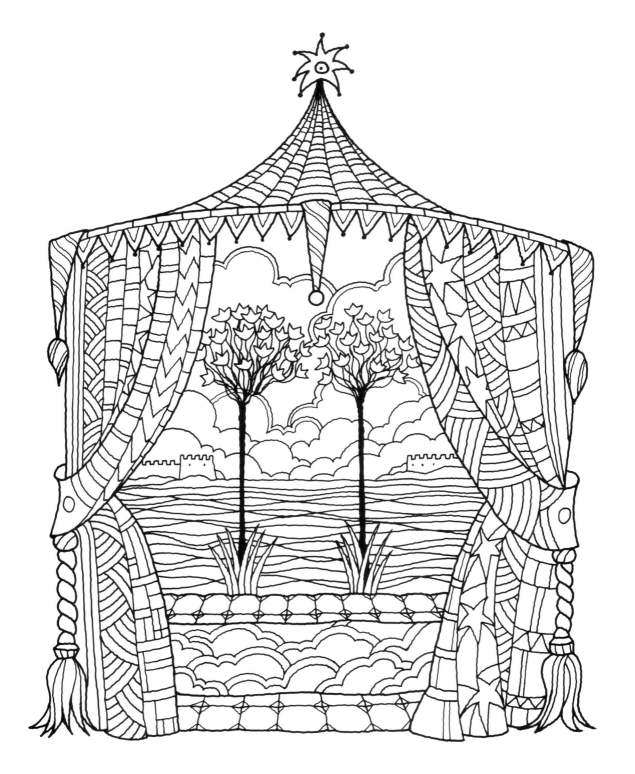

The Cloud Pavilion

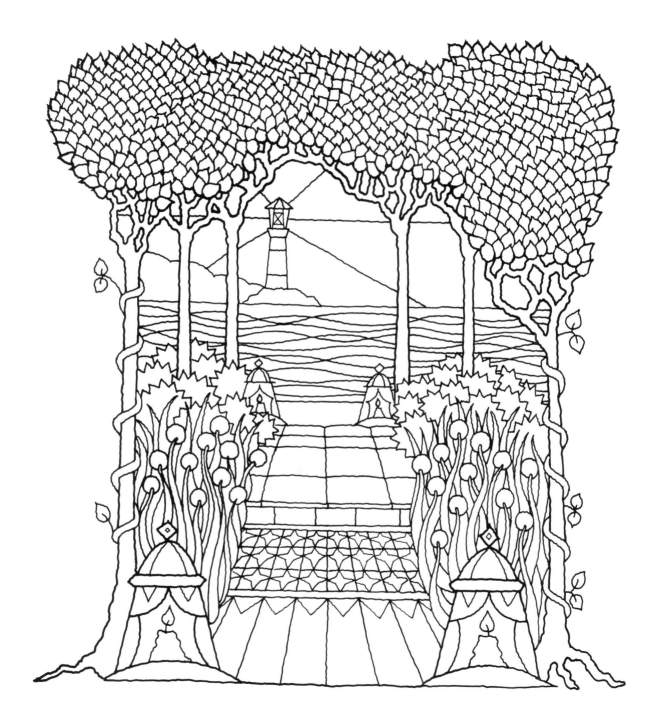

The Lantern Path

~The Hidden Doorway~

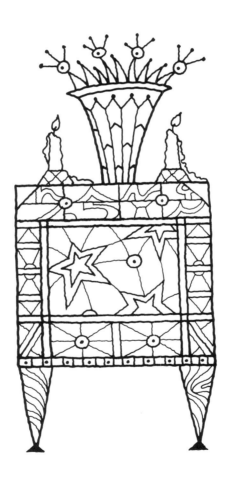

The Alchemist's Alcove

The Shell Grotto

The Midday Tables

~The Three Towers~

~The River Walk~

The Boathouse Folly

The Star Garden

The Casket of Jewels

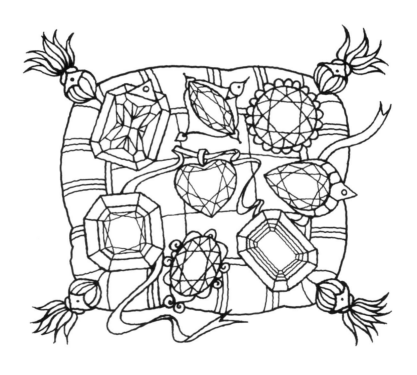

The Closet of Silks

The Evening Library

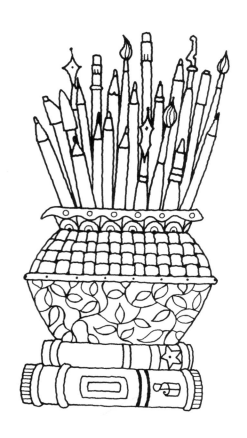

~The Moon Window~

The Night Stairs

~The Second-best Bed~

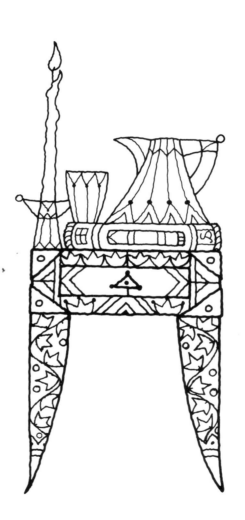

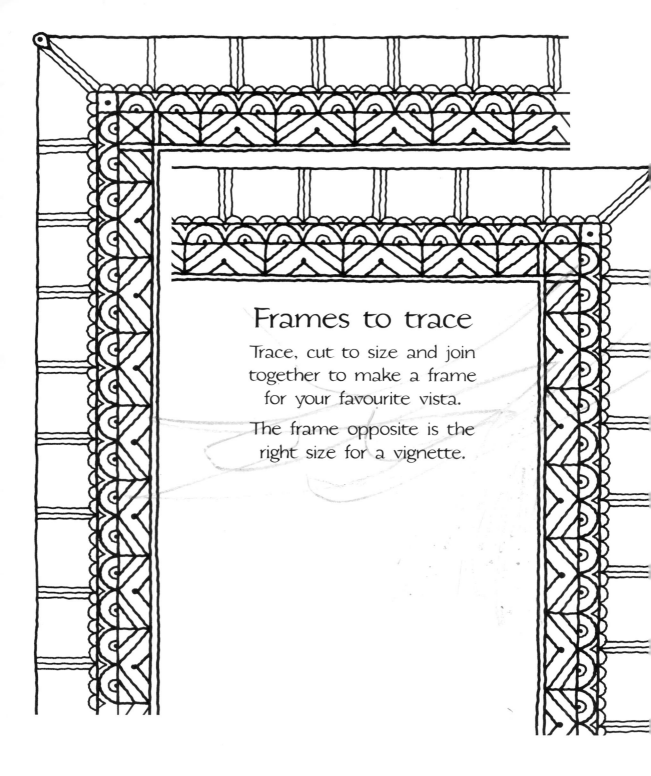

Frames to trace

Trace, cut to size and join
together to make a frame
for your favourite vista.

The frame opposite is the
right size for a vignette.

Test your pens here

This is where you find out if the colour from your marker pens shows through on the other side of the paper.

❖

Discover the BOHemians,
the Book of Hours community,
at
www.septimus-press.com

❖

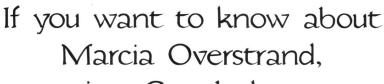

If you want to know about
Marcia Overstrand,
just Google her.

❖

GW00319910

love Doughnuts

Discover deliciously divine doughnut recipes

First published in 2013
LOVE FOOD is an imprint of Parragon Books Ltd

Parragon
Chartist House
15-17 Trim Street
Bath, BA1 1HA

ISBN: 978-1-4723-0204-5

Printed in China

Photography by Mike Cooper
Home economy by Sumi Glass
New recipes and introduction by Angela Drake
Edited by Fiona Biggs

Notes for the Reader
This book uses both metric and imperial measurements. Follow the same units of measurement throughout; do not mix metric and
imperial. All spoon measurements are level: teaspoons are assumed to be 5 ml, and tablespoons are assumed to be 15 ml. Unless
otherwise stated, milk is assumed to be full fat, eggs and individual vegetables are medium, and pepper is freshly ground black
pepper. Unless otherwise stated, all root vegetables should be washed in plain water and peeled prior to using.

Garnishes, decorations and serving suggestions are all optional and not necessarily included in the recipe ingredients or method. The
times given are an approximate guide only. Preparation times differ according to the techniques used by different people and the
cooking times may also vary from those given. Optional ingredients, variations or serving suggestions have not been included in the
time calculations.

Recipes using raw or very lightly cooked eggs should be avoided by infants, the elderly, pregnant women, convalescents and anyone
suffering from an illness. Pregnant and breastfeeding women are advised to avoid eating peanuts and peanut products. Sufferers from
nut allergies should be aware that some of the ready-made ingredients used in the recipes in this book may contain nuts. Always
check the packaging before use. Vegetarians should be aware that some of the ready-made ingredients used in the recipes in this
book may contain animal products. Always check the packaging before use.

Contents

Divine Doughnuts

Smothered in a delicious sticky sweet glaze, dipped in chocolate, filled with cream, custard or jam or simply warm and dusted with sugar. Freshly made doughnuts are the ultimate sweet treat - probably not a daily one but certainly an extra-special one. This book is full of all you need to know about doughnuts, with 32 recipes from around the world including all the classics as well as baked doughnuts, cake doughnuts and savoury ones too!
So why not indulge family and friends and have a go at one or more of these fabulous doughnut recipes? You'll be surprised at just how easy they are to make!

TYPES OF DOUGHNUTS

YEAST – these are the most popular types of doughnuts. They are made with soft bread dough, usually lightly sweetened with sugar. The dough is kneaded until smooth and left in a warm place to rise before shaping and frying to get that wonderful light and open texture. This type of dough is nearly always fried.

CAKE – a quick and easy cake mixture is used to make these doughnuts. There's no need to knead the dough or leave it to rise, simply roll it out, shape it and fry. This type of mixture will result in a doughnut with a closer texture than a yeasted doughnut and a crispier crust.

BAKED CAKE – a light cake batter is used for this type of doughnut. To get the perfect ring doughnut shape you will need to invest in a doughnut tray (see essential equipment). These doughnuts have a much lighter sponge cake texture but they are quick to make, will keep for 2–3 days and are less calorific than fried doughnuts.

CHURROS – made with choux pastry dough which is usually either piped or dropped into hot oil for frying. This type of doughnut has a much lighter and more open texture than yeast or cake doughnuts. They take just minutes to make and cook – perfect when you want that fried doughnut fix.

ESSENTIAL EQUIPMENT

DOUGHNUT/COOKIE CUTTERS – if you plan to make lots of ring doughnuts it's worth buying a doughnut cutter. This handy gadget stamps the doughnut shape in one swift action. But it's almost as easy to use two round cookie cutters – one about 8 cm/3¼ inches diameter and one measuring about 2.5 cm/1 inch to cut out the holes.

LARGE DEEP PAN OR DEEP-FRYER – a deep-fryer with a built-in temperature gauge makes frying doughnuts really easy, however there's no need to rush out and buy one. A good-sized, heavy-based deep pan that can be filled to an 8-cm/3¼-inch depth with oil is perfectly suitable and easier to clean.

STAND MIXER – a stand mixer helps to make light work out of doughnut-making. They come with a paddle attachment for mixing and a dough hook for kneading.

THERMOMETER – a sugar thermometer will ensure that you heat the oil to the correct temperature for frying. It needs to be made of brass or metal and measure up to a temperature of at least 200°C/400°F.

DOUGHNUT PANS – for baked cake doughnuts you'll need a doughnut tray that has 6 or 12 moulded doughnut ring-shaped dips. The mixture is then piped or spooned into the dips before baking in the oven. You can also buy mini doughnut pans – ideal for bite-sized sweet treats.

PIPING BAG AND NOZZLES – for piping churros into hot oil or filling doughnut trays with batter a large piping bag is useful. Buy a reusable plastic bag or a roll of sturdy disposable bags. A few different sized plain and fluted nozzles are handy too.

ESSENTIAL INGREDIENTS

You only need a few ingredients for most of the recipes in this book. Here's a guide to some of the basics...

EASY-BLEND DRIED YEAST – unlike fresh or ordinary dried yeast that has to be activated in warm sweetened liquid before adding to the dry ingredients, easy-blend (or fast action) yeast is just stirred into the flour. If you use ordinary dried yeast then mix it with some of the warm liquid and sugar or honey from the recipe and leave for 15 minutes until frothy before adding it to the flour with the rest of the liquid.

FLOUR – for yeast-based doughnuts it's vital to use a strong plain flour with a high gluten content. This allows the dough to be kneaded and stretched and will result in a light and airy textured doughnut. For cake and baked doughnuts use either plain or self-raising flour with baking powder or bicarbonate of soda as the raising agent.

SUGAR – caster sugar which has a fine texture that dissolves easily is best for sweetening the doughnut mixture, but caster, granulated or icing sugar can be used to coat the warm cooked doughnuts.

OIL – choose a light flavourless oil that can be heated to a high temperature for frying the doughnuts. Sunflower, peanut or good quality vegetable oil are all fine. You can use the same oil for two–three batches of frying but always strain after each use and discard the oil when it starts to turn a darker colour.

EGGS – eggs enrich yeast dough and are essential for a cake or baked dough. Allow to come to room temperature before using.

TIPS FOR MAKING YEAST DOUGH

- Don't overheat the liquid – it should be quite warm but not too hot or it will kill the yeast and the dough won't rise.
- It's better to have a soft, sticky dough and gradually incorporate more flour than a dry and crumbly dough which will be hard to knead and take longer to rise.
- Once the doughnuts have been shaped, don't leave them for too long before frying as they can over-prove and lose their shape.

TIPS FOR FRYING DOUGHNUTS

- If you are using a pan of oil don't over-fill it – there should be at least 5 cm/2 inches from the top of the oil to the rim of the pan.
- It's essential to maintain the correct temperature when frying the doughnuts. If the temperature is too high they will overbrown but not cook through. If it's too low the doughnuts will take longer to cook and absorb more oil making them soggy and fatty.
- Don't overcrowd the fryer or pan with doughnuts as this will reduce the temperature of the oil.
- Never leave hot oil unattended as it can be dangerous.

TIPS FOR BAKING DOUGHNUTS

- Thoroughly grease the doughnut pan before use with either softened or melted butter or a cooking spray.
- Don't overfill the rings or you'll lose the doughnut shape during baking. Piping the mixture is the best way to evenly fill the tray, but if the mixture has fruit in it then carefully spoon it in with a teaspoon, wiping away any spills with kitchen paper.
- Take care not to over-cook baked doughnuts or they will have a dry texture. The doughnuts should just spring back when lightly pressed with your fingertips.

Simple Doughnuts

MAKES **PREP** **COOK**
12 45 25 MINUTES
PLUS RISING & CHILLING

INGREDIENTS

225 ml/8 fl oz milk

3 tbsp easy-blend
dried yeast

250 g/9 oz plain flour,
plus extra for dusting

2 tbsp caster sugar

½ tsp salt

3 egg yolks

1 tsp vanilla extract

55 g/2 oz butter, softened

oil, for greasing
and frying

GLAZE (OPTIONAL)

200 g/7 oz icing sugar

3–4 tbsp water or
full-fat milk

1. Heat the milk until lukewarm and dissolve the yeast into the milk. Add 200 g/7 oz of the flour into the mixture and set aside for 30 minutes.

2. Using a stand mixer fitted with a paddle attachment, add the sugar, salt, egg yolks and vanilla to the bowl and mix on a low speed until smooth. Add the butter and milk and mix slowly.

3. Change the paddle attachment to a dough hook and add the remaining flour. Mix slowly until the dough is smooth. Refrigerate the mixture for 1 hour.

4. Lightly grease a baking tray. Roll the dough on a floured surface. The dough should be about 1 cm/½ inch thick. Use a doughnut cutter to cut out the doughnuts.

5. Place on the greased baking tray, cover with clingfilm and leave in a warm place. The doughnuts should rise to nearly double the original size and spring back when touched.

6. Heat enough oil for deep-frying in a large saucepan or deep-fryer to 180-190°C/350-375°F, or until a cube of bread browns in 30 seconds. Carefully place the doughnuts, one at a time, into the hot oil. Fry for 2 minutes or until golden brown. Remove with a slotted spoon and drain on kitchen paper.

7. To make the glaze, place the sugar in a bowl and slowly mix in the water or milk until smooth. Pour over the cooled doughnuts.

Simple yet delicious, these classic doughnuts are the perfect treat, with or without the icing sugar glaze.

Jam Doughnuts

MAKES PREP COOK
10 25 25 MINUTES
PLUS RISING

INGREDIENTS

oil, for greasing
and frying

450 g/1 lb strong
white flour, plus extra
for dusting

55 g/2 oz butter,
cut into pieces

2 tbsp caster sugar

½ tsp salt

2¼ tsp easy-blend dried
yeast

1 egg, lightly beaten

175 ml/6 fl oz lukewarm
milk

FILLING

150 g/5½ oz seedless
strawberry or raspberry jam

1. Lightly grease a large bowl and 2 baking trays.

2. Place the flour in a large bowl, add the butter and rub it in until the mixture resembles breadcrumbs. Stir in the sugar, salt and yeast. Make a well in the centre and add the egg and milk, then mix to form a soft, pliable dough. Knead well for 10 minutes.

3. Place in the greased bowl and cover. Leave in a warm place to rise for about 1 hour or until doubled in size.

4. Knead the dough on a floured work surface, then divide into 10 pieces. Shape each piece into a ball and place on the prepared baking trays. Cover and leave in a warm place to double in size for 45 minutes.

5. Heat enough oil for deep-frying in a large saucepan or deep-fryer to 180-190°C/350-375°F, or until a cube of bread browns in 30 seconds. Deep-fry the doughnuts in batches for 2-3 minutes each side. Remove with a slotted spoon, drain on kitchen paper and dust with sugar.

6. To fill the doughnuts, spoon the jam into a piping bag fitted with a plain nozzle. Insert a sharp knife into each doughnut and twist to make a hole. Push the point of the nozzle into the hole and pipe in some jam.

Why not try blueberry or apricot Jam — or any other type of Jam you like — for a different taste experience.

Baked Ring
Doughnuts

MAKES **16** PREP **20** COOK **45** MINUTES

INGREDIENTS

225 g/8 oz self-raising flour
1½ tsp baking powder
175 g/6 oz caster sugar
½ tsp salt
150 ml/5 fl oz milk
2 eggs, beaten
½ tsp vanilla extract
40 g/1½ oz butter, melted,
plus extra for greasing

SUGAR COATING
4 tbsp caster sugar
2–3 tsp ground cinnamon

1. Preheat the oven to 190°C/375°F/Gas Mark 5. Grease a 6-hole doughnut tin.

2. Sift together the flour and baking powder into a bowl and stir in the sugar and salt. Make a well in the centre. Mix together the milk, eggs, vanilla extract and butter and pour into the well. Mix until smooth.

3. Spoon the mixture into a large piping bag fitted with a plain nozzle. Pipe some of the mixture into the prepared tin, filling each hole about two-thirds full. Bake in the preheated oven for 10–15 minutes, or until risen, golden and just firm to the touch. Leave to cool in the tin for 5 minutes, then turn out onto a wire rack. Bake the remaining mixture in the same way, rinsing and greasing the pan each time, to make 16 doughnuts in total.

4. To make the sugar coating, mix together the sugar and cinnamon on a plate. Gently toss each warm doughnut in the cinnamon sugar to coat completely. Serve warm or cold.

14

Made with a simple cake batter instead of yeast dough these baked doughnuts have a lovely light texture and will keep fresh for longer than deep-fried doughnuts.

Custard Doughnuts

MAKES **8** PREP **45** COOK **20** MINUTES

PLUS RISING

INGREDIENTS

175 ml/6 fl oz milk

25 g/1 oz butter

350 g/12 oz strong white flour, plus extra for dusting and kneading

½ tsp salt

1½ tsp easy-blend dried yeast

25 g/1 oz caster sugar, plus extra for coating

1 egg, beaten

oil, for deep-frying and greasing

4 tbsp seedless raspberry jam

FILLING

2 eggs

55 g/2 oz caster sugar

1 tsp vanilla extract

3 tbsp cornflour

450 ml/16 fl oz milk

1. Put the milk and butter into a small saucepan over a low heat and heat until the butter has melted. Leave to cool for 5 minutes.

2. Sift the flour into a large bowl and stir in the salt, yeast and sugar. Pour in the milk mixture and the egg and mix to a soft dough. Turn out the dough onto a floured surface and knead for 5–6 minutes, until smooth and elastic, adding a little more flour if needed.

3. Put the dough into a bowl, cover and leave to stand in a warm place for 1 hour, or until doubled in size. Line two large baking sheets with baking paper.

4. Knock back the dough and divide into 8 pieces. Shape each piece into a 13-cm/5-inch length. Place on the prepared baking sheets and cover with lightly oiled clingfilm. Leave to stand in a warm place for 10–15 minutes, until puffy.

5. Heat enough oil for deep-frying in a large saucepan or deep-fryer to 180–190°C/350–375°F, or until a cube of bread browns in 30 seconds. Add the doughnuts, 2–3 at a time, and fry on each side for 1–2 minutes, or until golden. Remove and drain on kitchen paper, then toss in sugar to coat. Leave to cool.

6. To make the filling, put the eggs, sugar, vanilla extract and cornflour into a bowl and whisk together until smooth. Put the milk into a saucepan over a medium heat and heat until almost boiling, then whisk it into the egg mixture. Return the custard to the pan and cook, whisking constantly, for 8–10 minutes, until smooth and thickened. Transfer to a bowl, cover the surface with greaseproof paper and leave to cool completely.

7. Split the doughnuts lengthways and spread jam down the centre of each one. Spoon the custard into a large piping bag fitted with a star-shaped nozzle and pipe the custard on top of the jam.

Split and filled with jam and a vanilla pastry cream, these doughnuts make the perfect tea-time treat. Replace the pastry cream with whipped cream, if you prefer.

Yum Yums

INGREDIENTS

175 ml/6 fl oz milk

25 g/1 oz butter

350 g/12 oz strong white flour, plus extra for dusting and kneading

½ tsp salt

1½ tsp easy-blend dried yeast

40 g/1½ oz caster sugar

2 tsp finely grated lemon rind

1 egg, beaten

oil, for deep-frying and greasing

GLAZE

175 g/6 oz icing sugar

4 tbsp lemon juice

1. Put the milk and butter into a small saucepan over a low heat and heat until the butter has melted. Leave to cool for 5 minutes.

2. Sift the flour into a large bowl and stir in the salt, yeast, sugar and lemon rind. Pour in the milk mixture and the egg and mix to a soft dough. Turn out the dough onto a floured surface and knead for 5–6 minutes, until smooth and elastic, adding a little more flour if needed. Put the dough into a bowl, cover and leave in a warm place for 1 hour, or until doubled in size. Line two large baking sheets with baking paper.

3. Knock back the dough and roll out to a 25 x 31 cm/10 x 12½ inch rectangle. Cut the dough into 16 short strips and tightly twist each strip 2–3 times. Place the doughnuts on the prepared baking sheets and cover with lightly oiled clingfilm. Leave to stand in a warm place for 10 minutes, until puffy.

4. Heat enough oil for deep-frying in a large saucepan or deep-fryer to 180–190°C/350–375°F, or until a cube of bread browns in 30 seconds. Add the doughnuts, 2–3 at a time, and fry on each side for 1–2 minutes, or until golden. Remove with a slotted spoon and drain on kitchen paper.

5. To make the glaze, mix together the icing sugar and lemon juice until smooth. When the doughnuts are just cool enough to handle, dip each one in the lemon glaze to coat. Leave to set on a wire rack.

These short twists of dough with a lemon glaze are simple to make. Don't worry if they un-twist a little when fried — they will still taste delicious!

Coconut Doughnuts

MAKES **12**   PREP **20**   COOK **30** MINUTES

INGREDIENTS

175 g/6 oz self-raising flour

1 tsp baking powder

115 g/4 oz caster sugar

¼ tsp salt

150 ml/5 fl oz coconut milk

1 egg, lightly beaten

25 g/1 oz butter, melted, plus extra for greasing

100 g/3½ oz desiccated coconut

5 tbsp seedless raspberry jam, warmed

1. Preheat the oven to 190°C/375°F/Gas Mark 5. Grease a 6-hole doughnut tin.

2. Sift together the flour and baking powder into a bowl and stir in the sugar and salt. Make a well in the centre. Mix together the coconut milk, egg and butter, pour into the well and mix until smooth. Stir in 25 g/1 oz of the coconut.

3. Spoon the mixture into a large piping bag fitted with a plain nozzle. Pipe half the mixture into the doughnut holes. Bake in the preheated oven for 10–15 minutes, until risen, golden and just firm to the touch. Leave to cool in the tin for 5 minutes, then turn out onto a wire rack. Rinse and regrease the doughnut tin and repeat with the remaining mixture to make 12 doughnuts in total.

4. Sprinkle the remaining coconut over a large flat plate. Brush the warm doughnuts all over with the warm jam and dip in the coconut to coat completely. Serve warm or cold.

These light-as-air baked doughnuts are brushed with warm jam, then smothered in desiccated coconut. To give them a nuttier flavour, lightly toast the coconut.

Apple Doughnuts

MAKES PREP COOK
16 40 20 MINUTES
PLUS RISING

INGREDIENTS

275 ml/9½ fl oz milk

40 g/1½ oz butter

500 g/1 lb 2 oz strong
white flour, plus extra for
dusting and kneading

½ tsp salt

2 tsp easy-blend dried
yeast

55 g/2 oz caster sugar

2 tsp ground cinnamon

1 large egg, beaten

1 large eating apple,
peeled, cored and diced

oil, for deep-frying and
greasing

GLAZE

140 g/5 oz icing sugar

1 tsp ground cinnamon

2 tbsp milk

1. Put the milk and butter into a small saucepan over a low heat and heat until the butter has melted. Leave to cool for 5 minutes.

2. Sift the flour into a large bowl and stir in the salt, yeast, sugar and cinnamon. Pour in the milk mixture and egg and mix to a soft dough. Turn out onto a floured surface and knead for 5–6 minutes, until smooth and elastic, adding a little more flour if needed. Flatten the dough, spoon over the diced apple and knead into the dough for 2 minutes.

3. Place the dough in a bowl, cover and leave in a warm place for 1 hour, or until doubled in size. Line two large baking sheets with baking paper.

4. Knock back the dough and roll out on a floured surface to a thickness of 15 mm/⅝ inch. Use an 8-cm/3¼-inch round cutter to stamp out 12 doughnuts. Lightly re-knead the trimmings, roll out and stamp out another 4 doughnuts. Place the doughnuts on the prepared baking sheets and cover with lightly oiled clingfilm. Leave in a warm place for 10 minutes, until puffy.

5. Heat enough oil for deep-frying in a large saucepan or deep-fryer to 180–190°C/350–375°F, or until a cube of bread browns in 30 seconds. Add the doughnuts, a few at a time, and fry on each side for 1–2 minutes, or until golden. Remove with a slotted spoon and drain on kitchen paper.

6. To make the glaze, put the icing sugar, cinnamon and milk into a bowl and mix together until smooth. When the doughnuts are just cool enough to handle, dip the top of each in the glaze. Transfer to a wire rack to set.

Chunks of sweet apple and ground cinnamon give these deep-fried doughnuts a wonderful spiced fruit flavour. They are best eaten warm, just after the glaze has set.

Beignets

MAKES **PREP** **COOK**
30 35 25 MINUTES
PLUS RISING

INGREDIENTS

100 ml/3½ fl oz lukewarm
water

2 tsp easy-blend dried
yeast

55 g/2 oz caster sugar

½ tsp salt

1 egg, beaten

175 ml/6 fl oz evaporated
milk, warmed

450 g/1 lb strong white
flour, plus extra for dusting
and kneading

25 g/1 oz white vegetable
fat, softened

oil, for deep-frying

55 g/2 oz icing sugar

1. Put the water into a large bowl and whisk in the yeast. Add the sugar, salt, egg and evaporated milk and whisk to combine. Stir in half the flour and mix to a smooth batter. Beat in the vegetable fat. Add the remaining flour and mix to a soft dough.

2. Turn out the dough onto a lightly floured surface and knead for 4–5 minutes, until smooth and elastic, adding a little more flour if needed. Put the dough into a bowl, cover and leave in a warm place for about 2 hours, or until doubled in size.

3. Heat enough oil for deep-frying in a large saucepan or deep-fryer to 180–190°C/350–375°F, or until a cube of bread browns in 30 seconds.

4. Meanwhile, knock back the dough and roll out on a lightly floured surface to a thickness of 8 mm/⅜ inch. Use a sharp knife to cut the dough into about 30 squares.

5. Add the squares, about 4 at a time, to the hot oil and fry on each side for 1–2 minutes, or until puffed up and deep golden brown. Baste the top of the beignets during frying by gently spooning hot oil over them – this will help them to puff up. Remove with a slotted spoon and drain on kitchen paper. Thickly dust with icing sugar and serve immediately.

These puffed up, pillow-shaped doughnuts generously dusted with icing sugar are popular in cafes in the French quarter of New Orleans.

Chocolate Cake
Doughnuts

MAKES **14** PREP **25** COOK **55** MINUTES

PLUS RESTING

INGREDIENTS

125 ml/4 fl oz milk, warmed

1 egg

1 tsp vanilla extract

30 g/1 oz cocoa powder

225 g/8 oz plain flour

½ tsp bicarbonate of soda

½ tsp baking powder

½ tsp salt

100 g/3½ oz caster sugar

25 g/1 oz butter

oil, for frying

GLAZE

40 g/1½ oz plain chocolate, broken into pieces

40 g/1½ oz white chocolate, broken into pieces

1. Blend together the warmed milk, egg and vanilla extract in a bowl.

2. Using a stand mixer with a paddle attachment, mix the cocoa powder, flour, bicarbonate of soda, baking powder, salt and sugar together. Add the butter and blend. Slowly add the milk, egg and vanilla. Mix until the batter is smooth and thick and resembles a biscuit dough.

3. Leave the dough to rest in the mixer for 20 minutes.

4. Roll the dough out on a floured surface. The dough should be 1 cm/ ½ inch thick. Using a doughnut cutter, stamp out 14 doughnuts.

5. Heat enough oil for deep-frying in a large saucepan or deep-fryer to 180-190°C/350-375°F, or until a cube of bread browns in 30 seconds. Carefully place the doughnuts, one at a time, into the oil. Fry for 2 minutes on each side, or until golden brown. Remove with a slotted spoon and drain on kitchen paper.

6. To make the glaze, melt each of the chocolates separately in heatproof bowls set over pans of simmering water. Coat the doughnuts, drizzling the chocolates in a pattern.

28

You'll find it hard to stop at just one after trying these utterly delectable doughnuts...

S'mores Doughnuts

MAKES **12** PREP **45** COOK **16** MINUTES

PLUS RISING

INGREDIENTS

150 ml/5 fl oz milk

25 g/1 oz white vegetable fat

300 g/10½ oz strong white flour, plus extra for dusting and kneading

¼ tsp salt

1½ tsp easy-blend dried yeast

2 tbsp caster sugar, plus extra for coating

1 large egg, beaten

12 small squares plain chocolate

48 mini white marshmallows

oil, for deep frying and greasing

1 small digestive biscuit, crushed

GLAZE

55 g/2 oz icing sugar, sifted

2 tbsp water

1. Put the milk and vegetable fat into a small saucepan over a low heat and heat until the fat has melted. Leave to cool for 5 minutes.

2. Sift the flour into a large bowl and stir in the salt, yeast and sugar. Pour in the milk mixture and the egg and mix to a soft dough. Turn out the dough onto a floured surface and knead for 5–6 minutes, until smooth and elastic, adding a little more flour if needed.

3. Place the dough in a bowl, cover and leave in a warm place for 1 hour, or until doubled in size. Line a large baking sheet with baking paper.

4. Knock back the dough and divide into 12 pieces. Roll out each piece to a 9-cm/3½-inch round and place a square of chocolate and 4 mini marshmallows in the centre. Gather up the dough to enclose the filling, tightly pinching the edges together to seal. Place on the prepared baking sheet join side down and flatten each doughnut slightly with the palm of your hand. Cover with lightly oiled clingfilm and leave to stand in a warm place for 8–10 minutes, until puffy.

5. Heat enough oil for deep-frying in a large saucepan or deep-fryer to 180–190°C/350–375°F, or until a cube of bread browns in 30 seconds. Fry the doughnuts, 3 at a time, for 1–2 minutes on each side or until golden. Remove and drain on kitchen paper.

6. To make the glaze, put the icing sugar and water into a bowl and beat together until smooth. Dip the top of each warm doughnut in the glaze and sprinkle over the biscuit crumbs. Serve warm.

The only way to eat these delicious
doughnuts is while they are warm
and the hidden middle of chocolate
and marshmallow is still molten.

Honey & Pistachio Mini Doughnuts

MAKES **PREP** **COOK**
24 20 20 MINUTES

INGREDIENTS

115 g/4 oz self-raising flour

½ tsp baking powder

pinch of salt

55 g/2 oz butter, softened,
plus extra for greasing

55 g/2 oz caster sugar

1 egg, beaten

6 tbsp milk

40 g/1½ oz pistachio nuts,
finely chopped

GLAZE

85 g/3 oz icing sugar

1 tbsp clear honey,
warmed

2 tsp milk

1. Preheat the oven to 190°C/375°F/Gas Mark 5. Grease a 12-hole mini doughnut tin. Sift together the flour, baking powder and salt into a bowl.

2. Put the butter and sugar into a bowl and beat together until pale and fluffy. Gradually beat in the egg, then stir in half the flour mixture. Beat in the milk, then fold in the remaining flour mixture and three quarters of the chopped nuts.

3. Spoon the mixture into a large, disposable piping bag. Snip off the end and pipe half the filling into the doughnut holes, filling each one about two-thirds full.

4. Bake in the preheated oven for 8–10 minutes, until risen, pale golden and just firm to the touch. Leave to cool in the tin for 2–3 minutes, then transfer to a wire rack. Bake the remaining mixture in the same way, rinsing and greasing the tin before filling.

5. To make the glaze, sift the icing sugar into a bowl and stir in the warm honey and milk to make a smooth glaze. Dip the top of each doughnut into the glaze then sprinkle with the remaining chopped nuts.

These dainty little baked cake doughnuts are
Just perfect for serving with afternoon tea.
You can replace the pistachios with walnuts or
hazelnuts, if you prefer.

Lemon Churros with Orange
Dipping Sauce

INGREDIENTS

100 g/3½ oz unsalted butter, diced

300 ml/10 fl oz water

140 g/5 oz plain flour, sifted

large pinch of salt

2 large eggs, beaten

finely grated rind of 1 large lemon

oil, for deep-frying

icing sugar, for dusting

ORANGE SAUCE

1 tbsp arrowroot

300 ml/10 fl oz fresh orange juice

40 g/1½ oz caster sugar

1. To make the orange sauce, blend the arrowroot to a smooth paste with 2 tablespoons of the orange juice and set aside. Put the remaining juice and the sugar into a small saucepan over a low heat and heat until the sugar has dissolved. Add the blended arrowroot and simmer gently, stirring constantly, for 4–5 minutes, until just thickened. Remove from the heat, cover and keep warm.

2. Put the butter and water into a large saucepan over a medium heat and heat until the butter has melted. Bring to the boil, remove from the heat and tip in the flour and salt. Beat thoroughly until the mixture is smooth and comes away from the side of the pan. Leave to cool for 5 minutes, then gradually beat in the eggs to make a thick and glossy paste. Beat in the lemon rind.

3. Heat enough oil for deep-frying in a large saucepan or deep-fryer to 180–190°C/350–375°F, or until a cube of bread browns in 30 seconds. Spoon the paste into a large piping bag fitted with a large star nozzle and pipe 4–5 short loops of the paste into the hot oil. Fry, turning frequently, for 2–3 minutes, until crisp and golden. Remove with a slotted spoon and drain on kitchen paper. Keep warm while frying the remaining mixture.

4. Thickly dust the hot churros with icing sugar and serve immediately with the orange sauce for dipping.

The tangy lemon flavouring ensures
that these warm Mexican-style
doughnuts are not too sweet, even with
a generous dusting of icing sugar.

Chocolate-coated
Doughnut Holes

MAKES	PREP	COOK
45	**40**	**20** MINUTES

PLUS RISING

INGREDIENTS

175 ml/6 fl oz milk

40 g/1½ oz butter

300 g/10½ oz strong white flour, plus extra for dusting and kneading

1 tbsp cocoa powder

2 tsp ground cinnamon

¼ tsp salt

1½ tsp easy-blend dried yeast

2 tbsp caster sugar

1 large egg, beaten

oil, for deep-frying and greasing

140 g/5 oz plain chocolate, broken into pieces

140 g/5 oz white chocolate, broken into pieces

chocolate vermicelli or hundreds and thousands, to decorate (optional)

1. Put the milk and butter into a small saucepan over a low heat and heat until the butter has melted. Leave to cool for 5 minutes.

2. Sift together the flour and cocoa powder into a large bowl and stir in the cinnamon, salt, yeast and sugar. Pour in the milk mixture and the egg and mix to a soft dough. Turn out the dough onto a floured surface and knead for 5–6 minutes, until smooth and elastic, adding a little more flour if needed.

3. Put the dough into a bowl, cover and leave in a warm place for 1 hour, or until doubled in size. Line three baking sheets with baking paper.

4. Knock back the dough and roll out on a lightly floured surface to a thickness of 15 mm/⅝ inch. Using a 2.5-cm/1-inch cookie cutter, stamp out about 45 rounds, re-rolling the dough as necessary. Place the rounds on two of the prepared baking sheets and cover with lightly oiled clingfilm. Leave to stand in a warm place for 5–10 minutes, until puffy.

5. Heat enough oil for deep-frying in a large saucepan or deep-fryer to 180–190°C/350–375°F, or until a cube of bread browns in 30 seconds. Add the rounds, 6–8 at a time, and fry for 2–3 minutes until golden, gently turning them in the hot oil all the time. Remove with a slotted spoon and drain on kitchen paper. Leave to cool.

6. Put the plain chocolate and white chocolate into two separate heatproof bowls set over saucepans of simmering water and heat until melted. Leave to cool for 5 minutes, then dip half the doughnut holes in plain chocolate to completely coat and dip the remaining holes in white chocolate. Top with chocolate vermicelli or hundreds and thousands, if using. Transfer to the remaining prepared baking sheet and leave to set.

36

For some the best bit of the doughnut is the hole — so why not just make a whole batch of them? These chocolate-coated ones are perfect for a children's party.

Baked Blueberry
Doughnuts

MAKES	PREP	COOK
12	**20**	**30** MINUTES

INGREDIENTS

200 g/7 oz self-raising flour
1 tsp baking powder
115 g/4 oz caster sugar
¼ tsp salt
125 ml/4 fl oz buttermilk
2 large eggs, beaten
½ tsp vanilla extract
25 g/1 oz butter, melted,
plus extra for greasing
125 g/4½ oz small fresh
blueberries

GLAZE

115 g/4 oz icing sugar
2 tbsp milk
1 tsp vanilla extract

1. Preheat the oven to 190°C/375°F/Gas Mark 5. Grease a 6-hole doughnut tin.

2. Sift together the flour and baking powder into a bowl and stir in the sugar and salt. Make a well in the centre. Put the buttermilk, eggs, vanilla extract and melted butter into a jug, mix together and pour into the well. Mix until smooth, then gently fold in the blueberries.

3. Using a teaspoon, carefully spoon half the mixture into the prepared tin, taking care not to overfill the holes – they should be about two-thirds full. Bake in the preheated oven for 12–15 minutes, or until risen, golden and just firm to the touch. Leave to cool in the tin for 5 minutes, then turn out onto a wire rack. Rinse and regrease the tin and repeat with the remaining mixture.

4. To make the glaze, sift the icing sugar into a bowl and beat in the milk and vanilla extract until smooth. Spoon the glaze over the doughnuts, letting it run down the sides. Leave to set.

Full of plump fresh blueberries, these doughnuts have a wonderful fruity flavour, perfectly complemented by the sweet vanilla glaze.

Cookies & Cream
Doughnuts

MAKES	PREP	COOK
12	**45**	**20** MINUTES

PLUS RISING

INGREDIENTS

175 ml/6 fl oz milk

25 g/1 oz butter

350 g/12 oz strong white flour, plus extra for dusting and kneading

¼ tsp salt

1½ tsp easy-blend dried yeast

25 g/1 oz caster sugar, plus extra for coating

1 egg, beaten

oil, for deep-frying and greasing

4 tbsp seedless raspberry jam

FILLING

450 ml/16 fl oz double cream

70 g/2½ oz chocolate sandwich cookies

GLAZE

140 g/5 oz icing sugar

2 tbsp water

1. Put the milk and butter into a small saucepan over a low heat and heat until the butter has melted. Leave to cool for 5 minutes.

2. Sift the flour into a large bowl and stir in the salt, yeast and sugar. Pour in the milk mixture and the egg and mix to a soft dough. Turn out the dough onto a floured surface and knead for 5–6 minutes, until smooth and elastic, adding a little more flour if needed.

3. Put the dough into a bowl, cover and leave in a warm place for 1 hour, or until doubled in size. Line two large baking sheets with baking paper.

4. Knock back the dough and roll out on a lightly floured surface to a thickness of 1 cm/½ inch. Using a 9-cm/3½-inch doughnut cutter, stamp out 8 doughnuts. Lightly re-knead the trimmings, roll out and stamp out another 4 doughnuts. Place on the prepared baking sheets. Cover with lightly oiled clingfilm and leave in a warm place for 10 minutes, until puffy.

5. Heat enough oil for deep-frying in a large saucepan or deep-fryer to 180–190°C/350–375°F, or until a cube of bread browns in 30 seconds. Add the doughnuts, 2–3 at a time, and fry on each side for 1–2 minutes, or until golden. Remove and drain on kitchen paper. Leave to cool.

6. To make the filling, whip the cream until it holds soft peaks. Roughly crush the cookies and fold into the cream, reserving 2 tablespoons for decoration.

7. To make the glaze, sift the icing sugar into a bowl and beat in the water until smooth.

8. Halve each doughnut horizontally and spread the jam on the bottom halves. Spoon the filling on top of the jam. Dip each top half in the glaze and place on top of the cream filling. Sprinkle over the reserved crushed cookies and leave to set.

With a lovely sweet cream filling, these doughnuts are perfect for a special occasion. They can be made the day before and kept in the refrigerator overnight.

Rocky Road
Doughnuts

MAKES **8**   PREP **40**   COOK **20** MINUTES

PLUS RISING

INGREDIENTS

175 ml/6 fl oz milk

40 g/1½ oz butter

280 g/10 oz strong white flour, plus extra for dusting and kneading

2 tbsp cocoa powder

¼ tsp salt

1½ tsp easy-blend dried yeast

2 tbsp caster sugar

1 large egg, beaten

oil, for deep-frying and greasing

TOPPING

115 g/4 oz milk chocolate, broken into pieces

40 g/1½ oz unsalted butter

3 tbsp chopped mixed nuts

40 g/1½ oz mini pink and white marshmallows

25 g/1 oz glacé cherries, chopped

1. Put the milk and butter into a small saucepan over a low heat and heat until the butter has melted. Leave to cool for 5 minutes.

2. Sift together the flour and cocoa powder into a large bowl and stir in the salt, yeast and sugar. Pour in the milk mixture and the egg and mix to a soft dough. Turn out the dough onto a floured surface and knead for 5–6 minutes, until smooth and elastic, adding a little more flour if needed.

3. Put the dough into a bowl, cover and leave in a warm place for 1–1½ hours, or until doubled in size. Line a large baking sheet with baking paper.

4. Knock back the dough and roll out on a lightly floured surface to a thickness of 1½ cm/⅝ inch. Using a 9-cm/3½-inch doughnut cutter, stamp out 6 doughnuts. Lightly re-knead the trimmings, roll out and stamp out another 2 doughnuts. Place on the prepared baking sheet. Cover with lightly oiled clingfilm and leave in a warm place for 10 minutes, until puffy.

5. Heat enough oil for deep-frying in a large saucepan or deep-fryer to 180–190°C/350–375°F, or until a cube of bread browns in 30 seconds. Add the doughnuts, a few at a time, and fry on each side for 1–2 minutes, or until golden. Remove with a slotted spoon and drain on kitchen paper. Leave to cool.

6. To make the topping, put the chocolate and butter into a heatproof bowl set over a saucepan of gently simmering water and heat until melted. Stir until smooth, then leave to cool for 5 minutes. Dip each doughnut in the chocolate glaze and place on a wire rack. Top with the nuts, marshmallows and cherries and drizzle over any remaining chocolate sauce. Leave to set.

These indulgent chocolate doughnuts have a smooth milk chocolate glaze and are loaded with nuts, marshmallows and cherries.

Churros

MAKES   PREP   COOK
16 25 20 MINUTES

INGREDIENTS

225 ml/8 fl oz water

85 g/3 oz butter or lard, diced

2 tbsp dark muscovado sugar

finely grated rind of 1 small orange (optional)

pinch of salt

175 g/6 oz plain flour, well sifted

1 tsp ground cinnamon, plus extra for dusting

1 tsp vanilla extract

2 eggs

oil, for deep-frying

caster sugar, for dusting

1. Heat the water, butter, muscovado sugar, orange rind, if using, and salt in a heavy-based saucepan over a medium heat until the butter has melted.

2. Add the flour, all at once, the cinnamon and vanilla extract, then remove the saucepan from the heat and beat rapidly until the mixture pulls away from the side of the saucepan.

3. Leave to cool slightly, then beat in the eggs, one at a time, beating well after each addition, until the mixture is thick and smooth. Spoon into a piping bag fitted with a wide star nozzle.

4. Heat enough oil for deep-frying in a deep-fryer or deep saucepan to 180–190°C/350–375°F, or until a cube of bread browns in 30 seconds. Pipe 13-cm/5-inch lengths about 7.5 cm/3 inches apart into the hot oil. Fry for 2–3 minutes, turning frequently until crisp and golden. Remove with a slotted spoon and drain on kitchen paper. Keep warm while frying the remaining mixture.

5. Dust the churros with caster sugar and cinnamon and serve.

Served either hot from the saucepan
or cooled to room temperature,
churros make a delicious treat.

Powdered Doughnuts

MAKES **8** PREP **35** COOK **15** MINUTES

PLUS CHILLING

INGREDIENTS

250 g/9 oz self-raising flour,
plus extra for dusting

1½ tsp baking powder

½ tsp mixed spice

¼ tsp salt

55 g/2 oz caster sugar

1 large egg, beaten

100 ml/3½ fl oz milk

25 g/1 oz butter, melted
and slightly cooled

½ tsp vanilla extract

oil, for deep-frying

115 g/4 oz icing sugar, plus
extra if needed, for dusting

1. Sift together the flour, baking powder and mixed spice into a large bowl. Stir in the salt and sugar. Make a well in the centre.

2. Put the egg, milk, butter and vanilla extract into a jug, mix together and pour into the well. Mix to a medium–soft dough, adding a little extra flour if the dough is too sticky to handle. Cover and chill in the refrigerator for 30 minutes.

3. Roll out the dough on a lightly floured surface to a thickness of 15 mm/⅝ inch. Use a 7.5-cm/3-inch doughnut cutter to stamp out 8 doughnuts

4. Heat enough oil for deep-frying in a large saucepan or deep-fryer to 180–190°C/350–375°F, or until a cube of bread browns in 30 seconds. Add the doughnuts, 3–4 at a time, and fry, turning frequently, for 3–4 minutes, or until crisp and deep golden. Remove and drain on kitchen paper. Leave to cool for 10 minutes.

5. Sift the icing sugar into a shallow bowl and toss the doughnuts in it to coat thoroughly. Serve immediately, before the icing sugar dissolves into the warm doughnuts – if this does happen, just dust liberally with more icing sugar.

Delicious warm, crisp and golden fried doughnuts without having to wait for dough to rise — that's the beauty of these yeast-free doughnuts.

French Crullers

INGREDIENTS

55 g/2 oz butter
125 ml/4 fl oz water
2 tsp caster sugar
115 g/4 oz self-raising flour
large pinch of salt
2 eggs
1 egg white
oil, for deep-frying

GLAZE

225 g/8 oz icing sugar
4 tbsp milk

1. Put the butter, water and sugar into a large saucepan over a medium heat and heat until the butter has melted. Bring to the boil, remove from the heat and tip in the flour and salt. Beat thoroughly until the mixture is smooth and comes away from the side of the pan. Return to the heat and cook, stirring constantly, for a further 1 minute.

2. Leave to cool for 5 minutes, then gradually beat in the eggs and egg white to make a thick and glossy paste.

3. Line a baking sheet with baking paper. Spoon the paste into a large piping bag fitted with a large star nozzle and pipe eight 8-cm/3¼-inch rings of the paste onto the prepared baking sheet. Place in the freezer for 1 hour.

4. Heat enough oil for deep-frying in a large saucepan or deep-fryer to 180–190°C/350–375°F, or until a cube of bread browns in 30 seconds. Carefully remove the semi-frozen rings from the baking sheet, add to the hot oil in batches of 2–3 and fry on each side for 2–3 minutes, until crisp and deep golden brown. Remove with a slotted spoon and drain on kitchen paper.

5. To make the glaze, sift the icing sugar into a large bowl and beat in the milk until smooth. Dip the warm crullers in the glaze to coat completely and transfer to a wire rack to set.

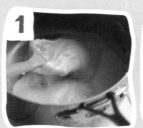

Crisp and golden with a sweet, sticky glaze, these yeast-free doughnuts are very simple to make. They are best eaten within a few hours of making.

Baked Pumpkin
Doughnuts

MAKES **6** PREP **25** COOK **15** MINUTES

INGREDIENTS

115 g/4 oz self-raising flour

½ tsp baking powder

½ tsp salt

1 tsp ground cinnamon

½ tsp grated nutmeg

50 g/1¾ oz butter, softened, plus extra for greasing

50 g/1¾ oz soft light brown sugar

1 large egg, beaten

1 tsp vanilla extract

1 tbsp milk

115 g/4 oz canned pumpkin purée

GLAZE

115 g/4 oz icing sugar

½ tsp ground cinnamon

2 tbsp milk

1–2 tsp maple syrup

1. Preheat the oven to 190°C/375°F/Gas Mark 5. Grease a 6-hole doughnut tin.

2. Sift together the flour and baking powder into a bowl and stir in the salt, cinnamon and nutmeg. Put the butter and brown sugar into a separate bowl and beat together until pale and creamy. Gradually beat in the egg, vanilla extract and milk. Fold in the flour mixture and pumpkin purée.

3. Spoon the mixture into a large piping bag fitted with a plain nozzle and pipe into the prepared tin. Bake in the preheated oven for 15 minutes, until risen, golden and just firm to the touch. Leave to cool for 5 minutes, then turn out onto a wire rack to cool completely.

4. To make the glaze, sift together the icing sugar and cinnamon into a bowl, add the milk and maple syrup and stir until smooth. Dip the top of each doughnut in the glaze and leave to set.

Smooth pumpkin purée gives these light baked doughnuts a lovely colour and delicious moist texture. For a spicier flavour use ground ginger instead of nutmeg.

Mocha Beignets

MAKES   PREP   COOK
24 **40** **20** MINUTES
PLUS RISING

INGREDIENTS

5 tbsp hot strong
black coffee

40 g/1½ oz soft light
brown sugar

1½ tsp easy-blend
dried yeast

¼ tsp salt

1 egg, beaten

125 ml/4 fl oz evaporated
milk, warmed

350 g/12 oz strong white
flour, plus extra for dusting
and kneading

25 g/1 oz white vegetable
fat, softened

oil, for deep-frying

2 tbsp finely chopped plain
chocolate

GLAZE

115 g/4 oz icing sugar

1 tbsp cocoa powder

1 tbsp cold strong black
coffee

1–2 tbsp milk

1. Place the coffee in a large bowl and whisk in the sugar until dissolved. Leave to cool for 5 minutes, then whisk in the yeast, salt, egg and evaporated milk. Stir in half the flour and mix to a smooth batter. Beat in the vegetable fat. Add the remaining flour and mix to a soft dough.

2. Turn out the dough onto a lightly floured surface and knead for 4–5 minutes, until smooth and elastic, adding a little more flour if needed. Place the dough in a bowl, cover and leave in a warm place for about 2 hours, or until doubled in size.

3. Heat enough oil for deep-frying in a large saucepan or deep-fryer to 180–190°C/350–375°F, or until a cube of bread browns in 30 seconds.

4. Meanwhile, knock back the dough and roll out on a lightly floured surface to a thickness of 8 mm/⅜ inch. Use a 5-cm/2-inch round cookie cutter to stamp out 24 rounds, re-kneading and rolling the trimmings once.

5. Add the rounds, about 4 at a time, to the hot oil and fry on each side for 1–2 minutes, or until puffed up and deep golden brown. Baste the top of the beignets by gently spooning hot oil over them – this will help them to puff up. Remove with a slotted spoon and drain on kitchen paper.

6. To make the glaze, sift together the icing sugar and cocoa powder into a bowl and stir in the coffee and enough milk to make a smooth glaze. Dip each warm beignet in the glaze and sprinkle with chopped chocolate. Serve immediately.

You can make the dough for these
doughnuts the night before and leave
it to rise slowly in the refrigerator
overnight, ready to fry in the morning.

Boston Cream
Doughnuts

MAKES	PREP	COOK
12	**45**	**20** MINUTES

PLUS RISING

INGREDIENTS

175 ml/6 fl oz milk

25 g/1 oz butter

350 g/12 oz strong white flour, plus extra for dusting and kneading

½ tsp salt

25 g/1 oz caster sugar

1½ tsp easy-blend dried yeast

1 egg, beaten

oil, for deep-frying and greasing

4 tbsp vanilla custard

100 ml/3½ fl oz double cream, lightly whipped

GLAZE

100 g/3½ oz plain chocolate, finely chopped

100 ml/3½ fl oz double cream

1. Put the milk and butter into a small saucepan over a low heat and heat until the butter has melted. Leave to cool for 5 minutes.

2. Sift the flour into a large bowl and stir in the salt, sugar and yeast. Pour in the milk mixture and the egg and mix to a soft dough. Turn out the dough onto a floured surface and knead for 5–6 minutes, until smooth and elastic, adding a little more flour if needed.

3. Place the dough in a bowl, cover and leave in a warm place for 1 hour or until doubled in size. Line a large baking sheet with baking paper.

4. Knock back the dough, divide into 12 pieces and roll each piece into a ball. Flatten slightly, place on the prepared baking sheet and cover with lightly oiled clingfilm. Leave in a warm place for 10–15 minutes, until puffy.

5. Heat enough oil for deep-frying in a large saucepan or deep-fryer to 180–190°C/350–375°F, or until a cube of bread browns in 30 seconds. Add the doughnuts to the hot oil, 3–4 at a time, and fry on each side for 1–2 minutes, or until golden. Remove with a slotted spoon and drain on kitchen paper. Leave to cool.

6. Use the tip of a small knife to make a hole in the side of each doughnut. Push the blade a little way in and move from side to side to create a space. Fold the custard into the whipped cream, spoon into a piping bag with a plain nozzle and pipe into the centre of the doughnuts.

7. To make the glaze, put the chocolate into a heatproof bowl set over a saucepan of gently simmering water and heat until melted. Put the cream into a small saucepan over a medium heat and heat until almost boiling. Pour over the chocolate and stir until smooth. Leave to stand for 5 minutes, then dip the top of each doughnut in the glaze. Leave to set.

Based on the classic American layer cake, these rich doughnuts are filled with sweet vanilla cream and have a rich dark chocolate glaze.

Maple & Pecan Doughnuts

MAKES **6**   PREP **45**   COOK **15** MINUTES
PLUS RISING

INGREDIENTS

125 ml/4 fl oz milk
15 g/½ oz butter
3 tbsp maple syrup
275 g/9¾ oz strong white flour, plus extra for dusting and kneading
¼ tsp salt
1½ tsp easy-blend dried yeast
1 egg, beaten
oil, for deep-frying and greasing
25 g/1 oz pecan nuts, finely chopped

FROSTING

55 g/2 oz soft cheese
40 g/1½ oz icing sugar
1 tbsp maple syrup

1. Put the milk, butter and maple syrup into a small saucepan over a low heat and heat until the butter has melted. Leave to cool for 5 minutes.

2. Sift the flour into a large bowl and stir in the salt and yeast. Pour in the milk mixture and the egg and mix to a soft dough. Turn out the dough onto a floured surface and knead for 5–6 minutes, until smooth and elastic, adding a little more flour if needed. Place the dough in a bowl, cover and leave in a warm place for 1 hour, or until doubled in size. Line a large baking sheet with baking paper.

3. Knock back the dough and roll out on a lightly floured surface to a 15-x 30-cm/6-x 12-inch rectangle. Use a sharp knife to trim the edges then cut into 6 strips. Place on the prepared baking sheet and cover with lightly oiled clingfilm. Leave in a warm place for 10–15 minutes, until puffy.

4. Heat enough oil for deep-frying in a large saucepan or deep-fryer to 180–190°C/350–375°F, or until a cube of bread browns in 30 seconds. Add the doughnuts, 2–3 at a time, and fry on each side for 1–2 minutes, or until golden. Remove and drain on kitchen paper. Leave to cool.

5. To make the frosting, put the cheese into a bowl and beat with a wooden spoon until soft, then beat in the icing sugar and maple syrup until smooth. Spread the frosting over the tops of the doughnuts and sprinkle with the chopped nuts.

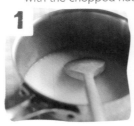

These Jumbo long doughnuts are perfect for sharing. For a quirky variation on the topping sprinkle with chopped crispy bacon instead of the pecan nuts.

Fudge Doughnuts

MAKES **8**   PREP **45**   COOK **25** MINUTES

PLUS RISING

INGREDIENTS

175 ml/6 fl oz milk

25 g/1 oz butter

350 g/12 oz strong white flour, plus extra for dusting and kneading

½ tsp salt

1½ tsp easy-blend yeast

25 g/1 oz caster sugar

1 egg, beaten

oil, for deep-frying and greasing

150 ml/5 fl oz double cream, whipped

FROSTING

55 g/2 oz butter

100 g/3½ oz soft light brown sugar

3 tbsp milk

1 tsp vanilla extract

70 g/2½ oz icing sugar, sifted

1. Put the milk and butter into a small saucepan over a low heat and heat until the butter has melted. Leave to cool for 5 minutes.

2. Sift the flour into a large bowl and stir in the salt, yeast and sugar. Pour in the milk mixture and the egg and mix to a soft dough. Turn out the dough onto a floured surface and knead for 5–6 minutes, until smooth and elastic, adding a little more flour if needed.

3. Put the dough into a bowl, cover and leave in a warm place for 1 hour, or until doubled in size. Line a large baking sheet with baking paper.

4. Knock back the dough, divide into 2 pieces and roll out each piece on a lightly floured surface to a 15-cm/6-inch square. Use a sharp knife to trim the edges, then cut each square into 4 smaller squares. Place on the prepared baking sheet and cover with lightly oiled clingfilm. Leave in a warm place for 10–15 minutes, until puffy.

5. Heat enough oil for deep-frying in a large saucepan or deep-fryer to 180–190°C/350–375°F, or until a cube of bread browns in 30 seconds. Add the doughnuts, 2–3 at a time, and fry on each side for 1–2 minutes, or until golden. Remove and drain on kitchen paper. Leave to cool.

6. Use the tip of a small knife to make a hole in the side of each doughnut. Push the blade a little way in and move from side to side to create a space. Spoon the whipped cream into a piping bag with a plain nozzle and pipe it into the centre of the doughnuts.

7. To make the frosting, put the butter and brown sugar into a saucepan over a medium heat and heat, stirring constantly, until the sugar has dissolved. Bring to the boil and boil for 1 minute, then stir in the milk and vanilla extract. Simmer for a further 1 minute, then stir in the icing sugar. Leave to cool for 10–20 minutes, until thickened. Dip each doughnut in the frosting and leave to set.

Popular as a sweet treat in Scotland these square doughnuts have a whipped cream filling and a delicious, sticky, vanilla-flavoured fudge frosting.

Soured Cream
Doughnuts

MAKES **24** PREP **20** COOK **40** MINUTES

INGREDIENTS

200 g/7 oz caster sugar

3 eggs

225 g/8 oz soured cream

1 tsp vanilla extract

450 g/1 lb plain flour, plus extra for dusting and kneading

1 tsp bicarbonate of soda

1 tsp baking powder

½ tsp salt

¼ tsp nutmeg

oil, for frying

GLAZE

200 g/7 oz icing sugar

3-4 tbsp water or milk

1. Beat the sugar and eggs together in a large bowl. Add the soured cream and vanilla extract. Mix well.

2. Add the dry ingredients and mix well again. Turn out onto a floured board and knead for 5 minutes. The dough should be fairly soft.

3. Roll out the dough to a 5 mm/¼ inch thickness. Use a floured doughnut cutter to stamp out 24 doughnuts.

4. Heat enough oil for deep-frying in a large saucepan or deep-fryer to 180-190°C/350-375°F, or until a cube of bread browns in 30 seconds. Cook the doughnuts, in batches, by dropping into the hot oil. Fry for 2 minutes or until golden brown. Remove with a slotted spoon and drain on kitchen paper.

5. To make the glaze, place the icing sugar in a bowl and slowly mix in the water or milk until smooth.

6. Pour the glaze over the cooled doughnuts.

This delightful recipe uses soured cream instead of milk, making them wonderfully light and moist.

Cream Cheese & Herb
Doughnuts

MAKES	PREP	COOK
16	45	20 MINUTES

PLUS RISING

INGREDIENTS

175 ml/6 fl oz milk

2 tbsp olive oil

350 g/12 oz strong white flour, plus extra for dusting and kneading

1 tsp salt

1½ tsp easy-blend dried yeast

25 g/1 oz finely grated Parmesan cheese

1 egg, beaten

oil, for deep-frying and greasing

FILLING

400 g/14 oz full-fat soft cheese

2 tbsp snipped fresh chives

2 tbsp finely chopped fresh parsley

salt and pepper

1. Put the milk and oil into a small saucepan over a low heat and heat until just lukewarm. Sift the flour into a large bowl and stir in the salt, yeast and Parmesan cheese. Pour in the milk mixture and egg and mix to a soft dough. Turn out the dough onto a floured surface and knead for 5–6 minutes, until smooth and elastic, adding a little more flour if needed.

2. Put the dough into a bowl, cover and leave in a warm place for 1 hour, or until doubled in size. Line two large baking sheets with baking paper.

3. Knock back the dough and roll out on a lightly floured surface to a 25-cm/10-inch square. Trim the edges with a sharp knife and cut into 16 small squares. Place on the prepared baking sheets and cover with lightly oiled clingfilm. Leave in a warm place for 10–15 minutes, until puffy.

4. Heat enough oil for deep-frying in a large saucepan or deep-fryer to 180–190°C/350–375°F, or until a cube of bread browns in 30 seconds. Add the doughnuts, 3–4 at a time, and fry on each side for 1–2 minutes, or until golden. Remove with a slotted spoon and drain on kitchen paper. Leave to cool.

5. To make the filling, beat together the cheese and herbs and season with salt and pepper. Slice the doughnuts in half horizontally and sandwich back together with the soft cheese filling.

These savoury doughnuts are great for a packed lunch or picnic. For a more luxurious filling add some slices of smoked salmon.

Cheese & Olive
Beignets

MAKES	PREP	COOK
32	**25**	**25** MINUTES

INGREDIENTS

100 g/3½ oz unsalted butter, diced

300 ml/10 fl oz water

140 g/5 oz plain flour, sifted

½ tsp salt

2 large eggs, beaten

6 black olives, stoned and finely chopped

2 tbsp finely chopped fresh parsley

3 tbsp finely grated Parmesan cheese

oil, for deep-frying

sea salt flakes, for sprinkling

1. Put the butter and water into a large saucepan over a low heat and heat until the butter has melted. Bring to the boil, remove from the heat and tip in the flour and salt. Beat thoroughly until the mixture is smooth and comes away from the side of the pan. Leave to cool for 5 minutes, then gradually beat in the eggs to make a thick and glossy paste. Beat in the olives, parsley and 2 tablespoons of the cheese.

2. Heat enough oil for deep-frying in a large saucepan or deep-fryer to 180–190°C/350–375°F, or until a cube of bread browns in 30 seconds. Drop 6–8 walnut-sized spoonfuls of the mixture into the hot oil and fry, turning frequently, for 4–5 minutes, until crisp and deep golden brown. Remove with a slotted spoon and drain on kitchen paper. Keep warm while frying the remaining mixture.

3. Serve the beignets warm, sprinkled with the remaining cheese and the sea salt flakes.

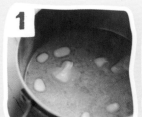

These light and crisp savoury doughnuts are made with choux pastry. Serve as a simple starter or canapé.

Cornbread & Pepper
Doughnuts

MAKES	PREP	COOK
6	**20**	**12** MINUTES

INGREDIENTS

15 g/½ oz butter, melted

1 tsp finely grated Parmesan cheese

70 g/2½ oz self-raising flour

1 tsp baking powder

85 g/3 oz fine cornmeal

½ tsp salt

¼ tsp pepper

1 large egg

6 tbsp buttermilk or natural yogurt

2 tbsp olive oil

1 spring onion, trimmed and very finely chopped

25 g/1 oz red pepper, deseeded and very finely chopped

1. Preheat the oven to 200°C/400°F/Gas Mark 6. Liberally brush the melted butter in the holes of a 6-hole doughnut tin, then sprinkle in the cheese.

2. Sift together the flour and baking powder into a large bowl and stir in the cornmeal and salt and pepper. Beat together the egg, buttermilk and oil and stir into the dry ingredients. Beat until smooth, then stir in the spring onion and red pepper.

3. Spoon the mixture into a piping bag fitted with a plain nozzle and pipe into the prepared tin. Bake in the preheated oven for 10–12 minutes, or until risen, golden and firm to the touch. Leave to cool in the tin for 2–3 minutes, then carefully loosen from the tin with a round-bladed knife. Serve immediately.

Perfect for serving at a weekend brunch, these
savoury baked doughnuts are easy to prepare
and take only minutes to make. They are best
eaten warm from the oven.

Chilli & Chocolate
Churros

MAKES **16**   PREP **20**   COOK **25** MINUTES

INGREDIENTS

100 g/3½ oz unsalted butter, diced

225 ml/8 fl oz water

140 g/5 oz plain flour, sifted

large pinch of salt

2 large eggs, beaten

½ small red chilli, deseeded and very finely chopped

oil, for deep-frying

4 tbsp sugar

2 tsp cocoa powder, sifted

CHOCOLATE SAUCE

85 g/3 oz plain chocolate, broken into pieces

100 ml/3½ fl oz double cream

½ tsp vanilla extract

1 tsp dried chilli flakes, crushed

1. To make the chocolate sauce, put the chocolate and cream into a heatproof bowl set over a saucepan of gently simmering water and heat until the chocolate is melted. Remove from the heat and stir until smooth, then stir in the vanilla extract and chilli flakes. Set aside and keep warm.

2. Put the butter and water into a large saucepan over a low heat and heat until the butter has melted. Bring to the boil, remove from the heat and tip in the flour and salt. Beat thoroughly until the mixture is smooth and comes away from the side of the pan. Leave to cool for 5 minutes, then gradually beat in the eggs to make a thick and glossy paste. Beat in the chilli.

3. Heat enough oil for deep-frying in a large saucepan or deep-fryer to 180–190°C/350–375°F, or until a cube of bread browns in 30 seconds. Spoon the paste into a large piping bag fitted with a large star nozzle and pipe four 10-cm/4-inch lengths of the paste into the hot oil. Fry for 2–3 minutes, turning frequently, until crisp and golden. Remove with a slotted spoon and drain on kitchen paper. Keep warm while frying the remaining mixture.

4. Mix together the sugar and cocoa powder on a flat plate and toss the warm churros in the mixture to coat. Serve immediately with the chocolate sauce for dipping.

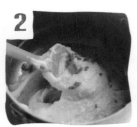

Chilli and chocolate make a surprisingly good flavour combination. So be adventurous and try these classic Mexican doughnuts.

Spiced Doughnut

Holes

MAKES   PREP   COOK

18   **20**   **20** MINUTES

PLUS RESTING

INGREDIENTS

125 ml/4 fl oz milk, warmed

1 egg

2 tbsp natural yogurt

1 tsp vanilla extract

225 g/8 oz plain flour

2 tsp baking powder

½ tsp salt

70 g/2½ oz caster sugar, plus extra for dusting

1 tsp grated nutmeg

25 g/1 oz butter

oil, for greasing and frying

1. Mix together the warmed milk, egg, yogurt and vanilla extract in a bowl.

2. Using a stand mixer fitted with a paddle attachment, mix the flour, baking powder, salt, sugar and nutmeg together. Slowly add the butter and blend. Slowly add the milk mixture until the mixture is smooth and thick and resembles biscuit dough.

3. Leave the dough to rest in the mixer for 20 minutes.

4. Heat enough oil for deep-frying in a large saucepan or deep-fryer to 180-190°C/350-375°F, or until a cube of bread browns in 30 seconds. Drop the dough, 1 tablespoon at a time, into the hot oil. Fry for 1 minute or until golden brown. Remove with a slotted spoon and drain on kitchen paper.

5. Sprinkle with caster sugar and serve.

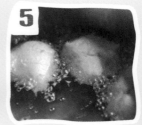

The nutmeg used in this recipe makes beautifully sweet and spicy doughnut holes — the perfect mini treat!

Vanilla, Cinnamon & Chocolate Doughnuts

MAKES **PREP** **COOK**
24 **60** **30** MINUTES
PLUS RISING

INGREDIENTS

300 g/10½ oz gluten-free, wheat-free flour blend

60 g/2¼ oz brown rice flour

¼ tsp xanthan gum

¼ tsp gluten-free baking powder

¼ tsp ground nutmeg

¼ tsp ground cinnamon

60 g/2¼ oz butter, softened

100 g/3½ oz ground almonds

½ tsp vanilla extract

1 egg plus 1 egg yolk

1 tbsp buttermilk

24 gluten-free dark chocolate buttons

150 g/5½ oz caster sugar, to dust

20 g/¾ oz ground cinnamon, to dust

oil, for greasing and frying

gluten-free chocolate sauce, to serve

YEAST MIX

10 g/¼ oz dried yeast

1½ tsp honey

1. To make the yeast mix, add 125 ml/4 fl oz tepid water to the dried yeast in a jug and stir in the honey. Leave to stand at room temperature for 15 minutes until frothy.

2. Sift the flours, xanthan gum, baking powder, nutmeg and cinnamon into a large bowl. Rub the butter into the flour mixture using your fingertips, until the mixture resembles fine breadcrumbs. Stir in the almonds, vanilla extract, egg, egg yolk and buttermilk. Pour in the yeast mix and stir well to form a dough, adding a little more water if required. Leave in a warm place until doubled in size.

3. Form 24 small dough balls and insert a chocolate button inside each one. Place them onto a baking tray covered in greased baking paper and cover with lightly greased clingfilm for 40 minutes.

4. Meanwhile, make the sugar dusting for the doughnuts by mixing the caster sugar and ground cinnamon together.

5. Heat enough oil to just cover the doughnuts in a large pan or deep-fryer to 180–190°C/350–375°F, or until a cube of bread browns in 30 seconds. Cook the doughnuts in the hot oil (3–4 at a time) for 2–3 minutes on each side until golden brown. Remove with a slotted spoon, drain on kitchen paper and roll in the sugar dusting. Serve with chocolate sauce.

These doughnuts are gluten- and wheat-free so
are ideal to make for guests with these dietary
requirements.

Cider Doughnuts

MAKES PREP COOK
12 20 35 MINUTES

INGREDIENTS

225 ml/8 fl oz sweet cider or apple juice

250 g/9 oz self-raising flour, plus extra for dusting

1½ tsp baking powder

1 tsp ground cinnamon

¼ tsp salt

55 g/2 oz soft light brown sugar

1 large egg, beaten

4 tbsp buttermilk

25 g/1 oz butter, melted and slightly cooled

oil, for deep-frying

55 g/2 oz granulated sugar

1. Pour the cider into a saucepan and bring to the boil. Boil for 10–15 minutes, until reduced to about 4 tablespoons of syrup. Leave to cool.

2. Sift together the flour, baking powder and half the cinnamon into a large bowl. Stir in the salt and brown sugar. Make a well in the centre.

3. Put the cider syrup, egg, buttermilk and butter into a jug, mix and pour into the well. Mix to a fairly firm dough, adding a little extra flour if the dough is too sticky to handle. Knead lightly until just smooth.

4. Divide the dough into 12 pieces and roll each piece into a ball. Flatten each ball in the palms of your hands to a thickness of 1 cm/½ inch.

5. Heat enough oil for deep-frying in a large saucepan or deep-fryer to 180–190°C/350–375°F, or until a cube of bread browns in 30 seconds. Add the doughnuts, 4 at a time, and fry, turning frequently, for 3–4 minutes, or until crisp and deep golden. Remove and drain on kitchen paper.

6. Mix together the granulated sugar and the remaining cinnamon in a shallow dish and roll each hot doughnut in the mixture to coat. Serve warm or cold.